The Illuminated Bile

# The Illuminated Bile

Poetry
*by*
Martin Tobias Lithner

Also by Martin Tobias Lithner

Reflections of Insanity (2011) – Deer Run Press

Ljus ur Intet (2012) – Akfeo Förlag

Trappsteg (2012) – Akfeo Förlag

The Illuminated Bile
Published by BoD 2014.
Copyright © Martin Tobias Lithner 2014.
Cover design by Martin Tobias Lithner.

Martin Tobias Lithner has asserted his right under the
Copyright,
Designs and Patents Act 1988 to be identified as the
author of this work.

ISBN: 978-91-7463-475-4

www.martinlithner.com

"Poetry is an echo,
asking a shadow to dance"

*- Carl Sandburg*

# PATH TO CLIMAX

Snake bitten by Medusa hair.
This silk embellished journey.
Stripped by her scornful smile,
the explorer gets a rough ride.

To reach the blood red ruby.
By all means, a walking dead
(weakened by serpent fever).
Fantasies, helps make it stiffer.

Inside the cave of sensitive flesh,
the ground began to tremble.
Wide open eyes can not hold
back the forbidden river.

In the moment of the cave-in,
the contraction of the muscle.
Buried beneath symbolic stone,
covered in pre-ejaculated fluid.

The laughing man is silenced by
the lack of moans, a questionable
performance & shrunken genitals.
Yet another path to climax ruined.

# SACRED IBIDES

Sacred ibides in flight.
Tears rolling down the
beak of Toth.
Eight principal deities,
leader of the Ogdoad,
now a punctured heart.

In a distance the Aquila.
The temples of Khmun,
burns so brightly.
Repudiate the oracular,
orders given concisely.
Death by fire, charred.

God of wisdom & the
moon, logos of Plato &
the mind of God, now
Latin words echoes
from the tongue of Ra.
A written afterthought.

# ASPERGIAN EYES

He weighed his own head in his hand.
Almost always made out of marble.
The sober meditation, can it be that he
pretends to be sunk in the deepest of
thoughts, a facade of internal struggle?

Do you truly represent philosophy,
intellect & poetry?
Dante in front of the gates of hell, or
did Rodin only form the bronze & marble,
to mock the absence of the thinking man?

Most of the observers ponder about the
hellish fate of those by Dante written.
The interpretation of Aspergian eyes,
is not he simply a man sitting?
A rhetorician can explain it better.

# DIVINE OSCILLATION

Four clocks upon my wall.
Each clock to remind me
of time wasted, time that
could have been used to
create. I envy those who
can enjoy the transition
of a slow minute.

In a queue of Neanderthals,
alienated as my evolved
eyes search for the next
movement, six degrees.
Listens for sounds of calm
tick tacking, hobgoblins
with Rolex wrist watches.

The intoxicating pendulum,
an ongoing hypnosis,
the resting equilibrium.
The chronophiles await the
completion of the first cycle.
They worship the mass less
rod & the divine oscillation.

Four clocks upon my wall.
Minute hands mock my lack
of commitment, my lack of
ideas, a state of osmosis.
Never comforted by the
words: "time is only what
a clock measures".

# DOWNBEAT CONCLUSION

At the threshold of chaos,
the rising rich read news
about the fifty thousand
(always in areas overcrowded).
Amplified skeleton hands,
created by media to reach
the encapsulated emotion.

How can we hold these hands,
if they already are guided
towards abiding darkness?
The pleas for the ever-starving.
I put money into this idea.
The true motivation behind
donation, a free, shinier soul.

The rich are grinning when
they are interrupted, focus shifts
from compassion to greed.
With dental white teeth they
explain to their kids that famine
is an African disease, the death
toll may exceed the bereaved.

Downbeat conclusion, bequeath
a portion of bittersweet fortune.
You may spread the word of your
deed, when you are dressed for a
celebratory evening. Empathy for
strangers, it always impress when
it is surrounded by a famous
seven figure radiance.

# THE WANDERERS

Wanderers of the news covered
valley, wanderers from strange
barren lands, look at your sisters,
look at them and you will begin
to understand.

Hardship & rapes outside of the
camp, movement without fuel.
Bartering for a better life in the
mud, barter for the life of a child.
Where is the balance?

Upon rich men platters, there are
leftovers worth millions, billions
of chances, trillions of thoughts.
Those who build towers aims
at breaking clouds.

A world of flickering light.

Is an increased awareness a
boon for the elated & his desire
for depression? Can we get
children with stuffed bank
accounts to join the rebellion?

## YELLOW AFTERNOON

Modus Ponens & the sun was shining.
She was left unsatisfied, grumpy with
cherry bubblegum & 3 dollar in her pocket.

She embarked on a journey, shorter skirt
meant longer ride, goldfish mouth & eyes
of prominent vacuum (high on antipsychotics).

She avoided green colored cars, red was her
lucky color, white haired men her lucky charms.
Tailored made floor mats, synthetic or handloom.

Button up, still three states to go (does she know).
On her back she spent an entire yellow afternoon:
"Have I crossed the river yet?"

# THE INFECTED

Pollution around the uterus.
Ideas creates an infected fetus.
We are no longer in need of
symbolic murmur, utterances
of false visions, paper wealth.

Should we allow these infected
to grow up without any claims?
Reaching the throne of wisdom.
Let them be advisors, standing to
the right (establish a rapid future).

The financial water slide creates
wretched images of tomorrow.
The last generation of infected
built these machines, but they
were never allowed into the
throne room.

The bursting of bubbles &
imaginary numbers, the hidden
subroutines, the hidden dreams.
Those whom are stuck inside the
pyramid screams: "Consume".

# THICK MYTHS

I do not care about the scales of gold or
the glimmering ecstasy that I have been
promised, insouciant ways threats the
Buddhist, the ephemeral genius hides
in darkness, waiting for his entombment.

Pegasus became glue, thick myths creates
hard lizard-like skin, above all this madness,
the pale virgin began to sing. The tobacconist
& the prophet, most often seen hand in hand.
The monoliths are all afraid of instant movement.

Fierce chicks do not miss a chance, invest in
youth, cotton candy pink, stupid sells, stupid fills
their pots of gold, but I still do not care, it is better
to never sell out to the masses, than to sell vanity
to the translucent.

# HOXTON SOULS

A white room, silver chandelier.
The black framed Madonna
explores your Hoxton soul.
The pale & freckled man thirsts
in the company of vibrant life,
a painting to capture each time.

Outside, the buzzing sound of
midnight, a whiff of rubbers &
massage oil, leather, skintight.
With blemished stretched skin &
bony shoulders, he shrugs when
asked: "Do death knock at arrival".

At the unisex hair salon they were
influenced by Caribbean style hair.
The barber was a simple man, from an
old & forgotten street, he changed into
high heels as soon as the sign turned.
These Hoxton souls, vital & suicidal.

Post-mortal preservation, a hobby
shared between these two, they built
a gallery of eyeless men, the skillful &
his disciple. All revealed in their grim
memoirs & by the postcards from the
Voodoo Queen of New Orleans.

# IMAGINARY VISIONS

Men who chase the dawn,
always rejects the night.
In their hunt of the light,
they become captivated
by imaginary visions of
the sun.

Their addiction can be
forgiven by the crimson
patrician & his pet friend,
the definition of a Christian
simpleton, but never by
the glistering logician.

# GREEN BOTTLE OF CHARTREUSE

Resting against a tombstone,
he marveled over the activity
in the grass, the language of
the birds & the noise of the
slumbering stream.

He was waiting for his love,
the definition of a vixen.
Like the 2nd law of motion
his thoughts accelerated by
the push from an eerie vision.

Bony hands dug up the mulch
& humus, the soil gave birth to
cracked skulls, soon there were
more corpses than in a sun-
drenched Ciudad Juárez.

Rattling of jaws created a
rhythmic beat, a skeleton dance.
Much like a childhood Halloween.
The monograph wrote itself, his
work was now almost complete.

There were no time for a lengthy
intermission, the play with the pen
continued, until his thoughts were
interrupted, she stood beside him,
with a green bottle of Chartreuse.

# GREENWICH CONFESSIONS

Feeling deliciously avant garde.
An apartment shared by five.
In the strive for bohemia they
papered the walls w/ cardboard.
Pam obviously amused by the
memories of green thrill Sundays.
Smiling, but with an absent shine,
the effect from the pills in her purse.
Stan, a former boyfriend to Pam,
danced around in his batik shirt.
Humming the choruses, written
before his birth.
Rehearsed poses & lush replies,
gave the twins a mysterious aura.
Named Liza & Mawu they were as
different as the sun is to the moon.
Vertical striped shirt & a purple tie,
yellow pants & a maroon felt fedora.
Juan loved to tease his friends,
A persistent Puerto Rican trickster.
The thought that their existence, is but
an exaggerated escape from the normal,
caused them to once again, act the
roles as the teenage rebels.
With gathered strength they revolted
against the electric company, bonfire
in the kitchen, activated sprinkler.
A feast of five, Greenwich confessions.

# TOWERS OF GLASS

Honeys with million dollar bodies.
Look at them, see how easy they
ride the light of flashing white.

Trained to walk, sixty meters.
Twist and turn, expressions sells.
This is my dearest & loving mum.

Family photos in Vanity Fair, styled
hair & sprained ankles, who cares?
With the pain comes concentration.

Next session, Jesus & his donkey.
The palm leaves must be gay erotic
black, your lips, red as lush poppies.

Our Mecca is Paris, Rue du Faubourg
& its luxury brands, lead by the Zodiac,
the nymphomaniac & her follies.

Must draw inspiration from the towers
of glass, how else can you portray a
raped & beaten Virgin Mary?

How did you end up on the front cover?
She remembers the hours of torture sex
with faceless friends of colleagues.

# LATIN PALINDROME

We go wandering at night
& are consumed by fire.
Constrained writing teach
us to impose beautiful
patterns.

The backward movement of
crabs, an esthetic experience.
The Latin palindrome, inked
in blood, rich words for the
stragglers.

Chopped off, as sudden as
a wife's discovery, blood &
mutilation, to write about
the reality of others.
Questions without answers.

## MY SON
### (Dedicated to Dante)

I sincerely hope that my son,
never inherit the key to the
twilight kingdom, beyond the
locked door's cool finish, there
are only flames of hatred & evil.

I sincerely hope that my son,
find his own path towards true
& admirable wisdom,  that he
never is to lose himself in the
cathedral of either dawn or dusk.

I sincerely hope that my son,
never in the eyes of his children,
become a brusque, hollowed egoist.
A stone monument of erected vanity.
An obelisk of static values.

I sincerely hope that my son,
becomes true, that he never
search for shade in tall shadows.
That he becomes a bright, shining
star, autarchic, escaping all
tempting vacuum.

# CANDOR & DANDER

The Jesters dance in flames.
The symbol of all power
melts away, the servant
carries burning bouquets.

The crackling sound of fire,
charred memories reveal
a fierce battle, he was too
grandiose in his movements.

Wildly gesticulating, his words
could not express his anger.
The king had finally had enough
of this Transylvanian rudeness.

With royal steel, he cut down
the chandelier, instantly the
hand-woven carpets welcomed
the long subdued flames.

The advisors from Sibiu were
the first to be caught on fire,
a stench of garlic & moldy
bread (then the signed Charta).

The burning king yielded his
sword, the instrument of his
success, with a final effort he
wrote in the memoranda.

"I'm nourished by intrinsic anger. Anger that live inside the heart of men. Remember us, men of candor & dander, whom today will perish in flames".

# YANKEE LANDSCAPE

A New England meadow's
alluring foliage, a delicate
balance met our eyes, a trace
of the approaching autumn,
made me take seven photos
more.

To obscure the true beauty
that lies hidden in the horizon
& behind that wind caught
shampooed hair, she was
never the object for my focus,
never my aesthetic desire.

The movement of unsteady
heels on the muddy ground,
tested the longest of patience.
Was it worth letting her pose
in only her boots, an
embarrassment in this

picturesque,

Yankee landscape.

# SON OF THE CABALS

An authoritarian government.
They never let themselves be
overshadowed by the presence
of others, they impose their
presence, their propaganda.

They are grandiloquent, behike
cigars, Mister Omnipotent.
Experienced fingers move the
stakes, the scattered banknotes.
Their smile, as the black dahlia's.

Financial results of the $1^{st}$ quarter
are once again written in bold style,
but men of the new world order,
can only be reached by extravaganza
& black magic abracadabra.

Horned killers inside of ivory towers.
Their movement echoes down the aisle.
The paid slaves at the mahogany tables,
feverishly conjures with rounded totals.
Biting nervously on their nails.

As the world waits for their next
appraisal, the men of power dreams
about global domination, son of the
cabals, the un-fallen, hidden by
a clever mistranslation,

*novus ordo seclorum.*

# QUEEN OF THE BOLSHEVICHKI

The outdated girdle forced
her to take smaller breaths.
She was renowned as an
authoress of impressive depth.

With staring blue eyes &
 a rehearsed smile, the truth
could only be seen for
a brief second.

In these staring blue eyes,
the water combed financier
were lost. Drowned by
his own promises.

A man of wealth, the smile,
the most insidious smile ever
shown, he raised his glass &
 proposed a credible toast.

"For your beauty", the quiet
men remained rectifications
around the decorated table,
their eyes focused.

Her vision became blurred,
was it something in the drink?
Absurd thoughts before she
was submerged into dreams.

She dreamt of furred
hummingbirds & about
the reserved. About the
endless queues of ill faces.

In this dream, the birds
of many reddish tones,
told her the secrets of
the sweet tasting nectar.

She was awoken by the sharp
smell of peppermint, inked.
A wrinkled paper, with her
fingerprint lay beside her.

"Queen of the bolshevichki,
editor of Pravda, the Tsar
await you in his quarter",
she slurred "the oppressor".

With her blue
proletarian eyes,
she hinted at
the sarcasm.

# THE SEARCH

Trashcan baby, the forsaken bambino.
Raised by nuns of the Monte Carlo casino.
Millionaire at age twenty, seem to see
the face of God in the red dice's eyes.
He enjoyed his single shot of cappuccino.
in the attractive *quartiers* of Monaco.
Lace underwear, scattered over an ornate
fan palm floor, her name came with 5 stars.

"Can there be darkness in paradise?"
He asked the aged piccolo: "sure, if you
know where to look", the man swore:
"Search for it in dusky yards & topless bars".
He went out on a journey through the
social classes, dinned with happy guns
& black suited torpedos, his nickname
became the conquistador of lost passions.
But there was no darkness to be found,
only men & women of misfortune, broken
souls, a venus with heartbreaking secrets,
a thesis from a mad genius, were to look?
"When the sun reaches its zenith, when
the shadows crawl nearer, then take a
look into yourself, there you will find
what you have been searching for".

The words from the enlightened one,
rumored to only speak the truth.
Can it be true?

Darkness can not be found,
if there is already darkness in the heart of man.

Wild influences creates sharp images.
Bold men gets desirable women, one
balanced on the tip of an aeroplane.
Hand-crank operated machine guns,
fires verbal insults at the western wall.
The legerdemain was too inhumane.

The witnesses on the ground could
only gape in awe as he disappeared,
into the thicknesses of cotton clouds.
Diminished distance, sun-dazzled eyes:
"…and now to please the men", the
amplified voice proudly pronounced.

Like Faust the necromancer, they felt
like they entered into a covenant with
the devil, her stage name was profanity.
Under a heavy set sky & with the roar
of celestial engines above, the beat
become a seductive blend, pure sexual.

# CHIVALRY

We are drawn to darkness.
Yet we long to wander the
starfield, we are emotional
splitted by temptations of
masculine lust & feminine
rose leaf romance.

The medieval ideal, chivalry.
Long dead or simply not
matching our new society.
As strange as a vernacular
dialect, our words of love
are now digital tailored.

Those portraying starchness,
can no longer let their words
match their heartbeat, match
their deep burning passions.
Chivalry is truly dead, with
verbal grunts they prance.

Unseal, crudity & malignancy.
If they were to know how far
a gentle word would carry
them, give clarity to these
pretenders. Within their hearts,
there is a knight of longing.

# A SPELL UPON A SPELL

A spell upon a spell, neon lights reflected
in the black wet pavement. The Go-Go
dancers chain-smokes behind VIP fences.

Corpses piled in the back street allies.
Robbed of bling & family photos.
Fueled by bourbon & Persian lectures.

The rain keep washing away our sins.
The corner girls are all dressed in
masculine attraction.

A spell upon a spell, taxi headlights glows
as greedy eyes, taking the lightheaded tourist on
a nocturnal ride. But rain ruins all traces.

Abducted children inside of blue buses,
silenced by city noises. Pale comes morning,
shine its weak light upon forgotten places.

# BURGUNDY SHADES

Some would not call it
theft, if you took all of
what was left, of men's
once burning will.
Still, they arise from
these burgundy shades,
from the depths of
moldy cellars.

Their run-away youth.
These forgotten dwellers.
They are all in need of
the dire wind.
Still, they are fighting
against this headwind,
believing that colors
never fade.

If the will is lacking and
nature slackens, what are
born out of a man
without this will?
Still, they thrive to live
without this force.
The theft is accepted,
noted and mislaid.